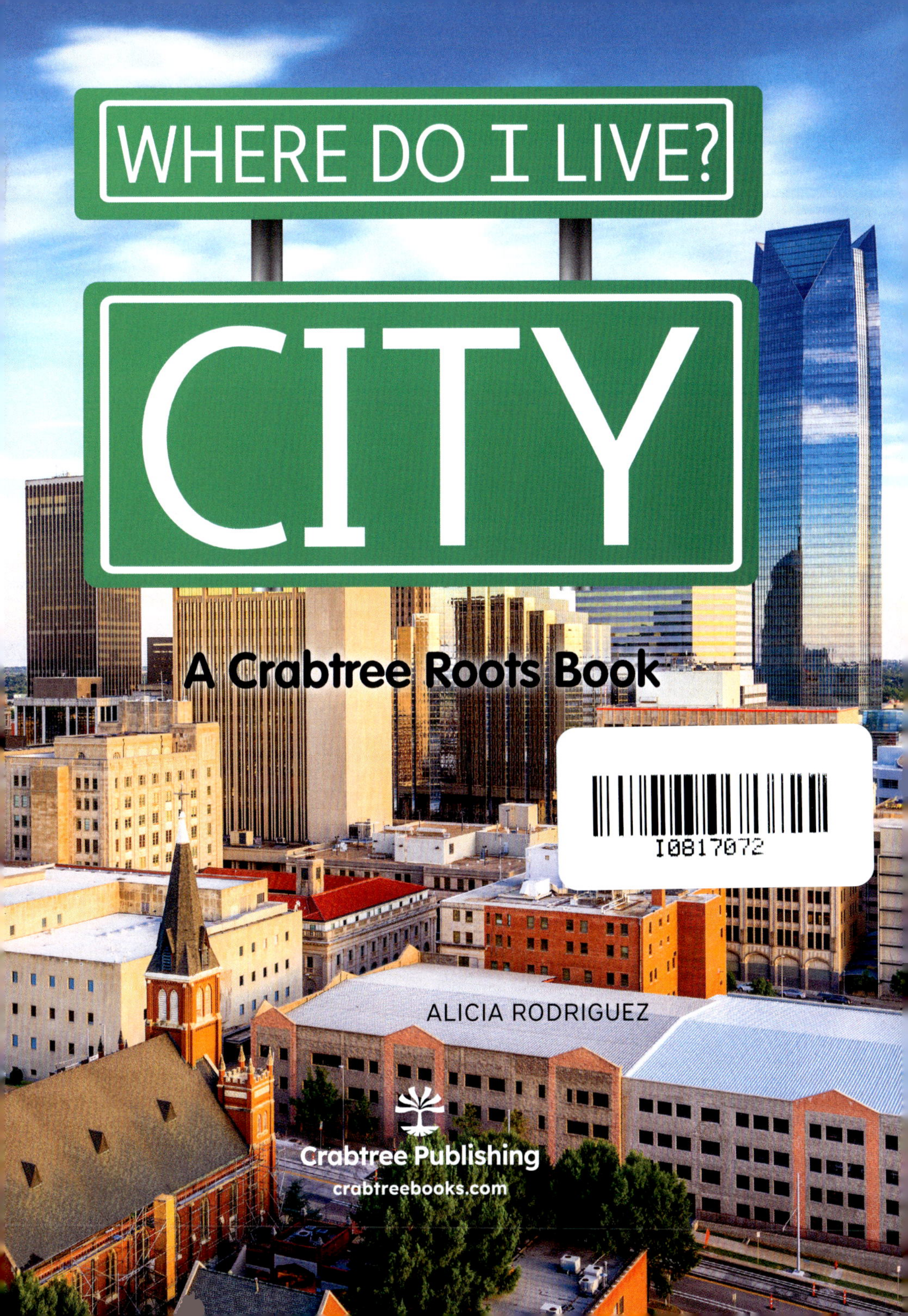

WHERE DO I LIVE?
CITY
A Crabtree Roots Book
I0817072
ALICIA RODRIGUEZ
Crabtree Publishing
crabtreebooks.com

School-to-Home Support for Caregivers and Teachers

This book helps children grow by letting them practice reading. Here are a few guiding questions to help the reader with building his or her comprehension skills. Possible answers appear here in red.

Before Reading:

- What do I think this book is about?
    - *I think this book is about cities.*
    - *I think this book is about what we can find in a city.*
- What do I want to learn about this topic?
    - *I want to learn how big a city is.*
    - *I want to learn what a city looks like.*

During Reading:

- I wonder why...
    - *I wonder why people walk to stores, parks, and schools in cities.*
    - *I wonder why it is fun to live in a city.*
- What have I learned so far?
    - *I have learned that cities have many buildings.*
    - *I have learned that cities have parks.*

After Reading:

- What details did I learn about this topic?
    - *I have learned that cities have schools.*
    - *I have learned that cities have tall buildings.*
- Read the book again and look for the vocabulary words.
    - *I see the word **city** on page 3 and the word **store** on page 8. The other vocabulary words are found on page 14.*

I live in a **city**!

I live in an **apartment**.

My friends live next door.

I walk to the **store**.

City Lights Bookstore
San Francisco
A LITERARY MEETINGPLACE SINCE 1953
3 FLOORS OF
BOOKS
OPEN 10AM - MIDNIGHT
EVERY DAY
CITY LIGHTS BOOKS

I walk to **school**.

I walk to the **park**.

I see tall **buildings**.

It is fun to live in a city.

Word List

Sight Words

a	is	see
an	it	the
I	live	to
in	my	walk

Words to Know

apartment

buildings

city

park

school

store

41 Words

I live in a **city**.

I live in an **apartment**.

My friends live next door.

I walk to the **store**.

I walk to **school**.

I walk to the **park**.

I see tall **buildings**.

It is fun to live in a city.

Written by: Alicia Rodriguez
Designed by: Rhea Wallace
Series Development: James Earley
Proofreader: Janine Deschenes
Educational Consultant: Marie Lemke M.Ed.

Photographs:
Shutterstock: fllphoto: cover; Sean Pavone: p. 1,3,14; Joseph ChunJr: 5, 14; Mike Dotta: p. 6; Nito: p. 9, 14; Christian Mueller: p. 10, 14; Majeczka: p. 12, 14

Crabtree Publishing

crabtreebooks.com 800-387-7650

Hardcover	978-1-4271-5998-4
Paperback	978-1-4271-6004-1
Ebook (pdf)	978-1-4271-3361-8
Epub	978-1-4271-3421-9
Read-along	978-1-4271-6022-5
Audio book	978-1-4271-6028-7

Published in Canada
Crabtree Publishing
616 Welland Avenue
St. Catharines, Ontario
L2M 5V6

Published in the United States
Crabtree Publishing
347 Fifth Avenue
Suite 1402-145
New York, NY 10016

Library and Archives Canada Cataloguing in Publication
Available at the Library and Archives Canada

Library of Congress Cataloging-in-Publication Data
Available at the Library of Congress

Printed in the